TIME TO WINE DOWN

An exclusive edition for

for all your gift books and gift stationery

This edition first published in Great Britain in 2018
by Allsorted Ltd, Watford, Herts, UK WD19 4BG

© Susanna Geoghegan Gift Publishing

Author: Michael Powell
Cover design: Milestone Creative
Contents design: seagulls.net

ISBN: 978-1-911517-38-2

Printed in China

TIME TO WINE DOWN

WHEN ONLY A TIPPLE WILL DO

WINE (NOUN): AN ALCOHOLIC DRINK MADE FROM FERMENTED GRAPE JUICE.

HOME BREW

—

If you squeeze some grapes into a jar and keep the mixture warm, it will turn into wine all by itself because of the yeast already present on the grape skins. The yeast will consume the sugars in the juice and produce alcohol. It won't taste very nice, but the first wine was probably created by accident in a similar way, more than 10,000 years ago.

EARLY WINEMAKING

—

Professor Patrick McGovern is the Scientific Director of the Biomolecular Archaeology Project for Cuisine, Fermented Beverages, and Health at the University of Pennsylvania Museum in Philadelphia. He pioneered the emerging field of Molecular Archaeology and is known as the 'Indiana Jones of Ancient Ales, Wines, and Extreme Beverages'. In 1996 he analysed residues from six nine-litre clay jars that had been found lined up in the floor of a mud brick Neolithic dwelling in Hajji Firuz Tepe in the Zagros Mountains in north-western Iran, twenty years earlier. He detected tartaric acid, calcium tartrate and resin and concluded that resinated wine had been made on the site as long ago as 5,400BC. It is the earliest chemical evidence of winemaking anywhere in the world.

EARLIEST CHEMICAL EVIDENCE IN EUROPE

The earliest chemical evidence of winemaking in Europe was discovered recently at the prehistoric settlement of Dikili Tash, in the Eastern Macedonia region of Greece. Ceramic vases have been excavated there containing the residue of thousands of carbonised grape pips and skins, dated to 4,200BC.

MASS PRODUCTION

The oldest site of the mass production of wine – the world's earliest winery – was uncovered by excavations, which began in 2007, of an ancient cave complex in Armenia known as 'Areni-1'. Archaeologists discovered ceramic storage jars and a large grape-treading trough which drained into a 15-gallon ceramic vat, as well as preserved remains of crushed grapes and vine leaves. The site is adjacent to dozens of graves, which suggests the wine was used for funereal religious purposes.

> WINE LOVERS KNOW THAT PUTTING SOME EFFORT INTO UNDERSTANDING AND APPRECIATING WINE PAYS BIG DIVIDENDS. SKILFUL TASTING UNLOCKS WINE'S TREASURES.
>
> Marvin R Shanken

ALL WINES SHOULD BE TASTED; SOME SHOULD ONLY BE SIPPED, BUT WITH OTHERS, DRINK THE WHOLE BOTTLE.

Paulo Coelho

WINE IS A PASSPORT TO THE WORLD.

Thom Elkjer

NOBLE GRAPES

Noble Grapes, also known as International Varieties or 'cépages nobles' in French, are those top shelf grapes that are grown in most of the major wine producing regions. Unsurprisingly, the original seven classics are all French, since France dominated the market for so many decades. They are: [Red] Pinot Noir, Merlot, Cabernet Sauvignon, Syrah; [White] Riesling, Sauvignon Blanc and Chardonnay. However, another 12 easily deserve to be added to any modern list today: [Red] Grenache, Sangiovese, Nebbiolo, Tempranillo, Malbec, Zinfandel; [White] Pinot Grigio, Chenin Blanc, Muscat, Gewürztraminer, Sémillon, Viognier.

TASTING NOTES: PINOT NOIR

Pale, translucent colour

One of the oldest grapes in the world, also one of the most expensive and difficult to grow. Low to moderate tannin (although some producers add tannins by using the 'whole cluster fermentation' technique, which allows the wine to be cellared for longer); crisp acidity. Aroma and mouth feel dominate. Often described as silky, satin. A fruity Pinot Noir will have flavours of raspberry, cranberry, black cherry and strawberry, but also light florals such as violet and rose petals. A complex expensive Pinot Noir such as Chambertin or Clos de Vougeot also contains rich earthy flavours such as mushroom, leather, game, truffle, wet leaves, even wild mint.

TUTANKHAMUN

Some of the earliest known wine labels were discovered in the tomb of King Tutankhamun, who became Pharaoh in about 1,333BC and reigned for less than a decade. Each of the 26 jars of wine was labelled in detail, for example: 'Year 5. Wine of the House-of-Tutankhamun Ruler-of-the-Southern-On, l.p.h. [in] the Western River. By the chief vintner Khaa'. Wine – predominantly red – was very important among the upper classes and rulers of Ancient Egypt, while the ordinary people drank low alcohol beer, although wine was occasionally given out as pay. In Egypt, the word 'wine' predates the word for vine, so the Egyptians must have imported wine long before they grew their own grapes in the Nile valley.

> THERE'S TRUTH IN WINE, AND
> THERE MAY BE SOME IN GIN AND
> MUDDY BEER: BUT WHETHER
> IT'S TRUTH WORTH MY KNOWING,
> IS ANOTHER QUESTION.
>
> George Eliot

SPEYER WINE BOTTLE

The 'Speyer wine bottle', or 'Römerwein', the world's oldest bottle of wine, dates back to between AD325 and AD350 and was found in 1867 near the town of Speyer, Germany, buried inside the stone sarcophagus of a Roman noble. The bottle was 'sealed' with a layer of olive oil and hot wax and has never been opened (although it would be undrinkable). It is currently on display at the town's Historical Museum of the Palatinate.

A GOURMET MEAL WITHOUT A GLASS OF WINE JUST SEEMS TRAGIC TO ME SOMEHOW.

Kathy Mattea

THERE'S A NEW WINE I WANT TO TRY. I HEARD ABOUT IT THROUGH THE GRAPEVINE.

Jarod Kintz

> **WINE IS NOT JUST AN OBJECT OF PLEASURE, BUT AN OBJECT OF KNOWLEDGE; AND THE PLEASURE DEPENDS ON THE KNOWLEDGE.**
> Roger Scruton

PRETENTIOUS, MOI?

In 2001, Frédéric Brochet, a PhD student at the University of Bordeaux, conducted a wine tasting experiment with 54 oenology students. He offered each wine expert two glasses, one containing red wine and the other white. In their tasting notes they used words like 'raspberry', 'cherry', 'cedar' and 'chicory' to describe the red wine, while the white wine was 'floral', 'honey', 'peach' and 'lemon'. In fact, the same white wine had been used, half of it dyed red. A similar experiment was conducted at the California Institute of Technology in which cheap wine was poured into expensive bottles and vice-versa. A panel of experts was unanimously fooled into favouring the cheap wine and brain scans revealed higher neural activity as well.

TASTING NOTES: CHARDONNAY

The most planted white grape in the world it may be, but choose the wrong Chardonnay and you'll be disappointed. So know what you like: oaked or not, buttery or crisp, zesty lemon (less ripe) or more tropical fruit flavours (more ripe). Chardonnay gets its vanilla notes and buttery, oily texture from the oak-ageing and an additional fermentation called Malolactic Fermentation (MLF) which turns malic acid into lactic acid. If you hanker for that creamy oaky butterscotch smoothness, choose a wine that has gone through MLF. If you enjoy a Chardonnay that has freshness, acidity and minerality, choose unoaked and feel smugly superior to all those crass acolytes of oak.

> THE MORE I HAVE LEARNED ABOUT WINE ... THE MORE I HAVE REALIZED THAT IT WEAVES IN WITH HUMAN HISTORY FROM ITS VERY BEGINNING AS FEW, IF ANY, OTHER PRODUCTS DO.
>
> Hugh Johnson

IN ITALY, THEY ADD WORK AND LIFE ON TO FOOD AND WINE.

Robin Leach

WHAT'S IN A NAME?

In 2011, a researcher at Brock University conducted an
experiment that showed that people are willing to pay
$2 extra per bottle if the wine has a name that's hard to
pronounce, regardless of the taste. Antonia Mantonakis,
Associate Professor of Marketing in Brock's Faculty of
Business, gave two similar test groups identical wine: one
labelled from the 'Titakis Winery', the other from the harder-
to-pronounce 'Tselepou Winery'. Subjects favoured the
'Tselepou' and participants who were supposedly more
knowledgeable about wine proved even more susceptible
to the linguistic trickery.

A BOTTLE OF WINE BEGS TO BE SHARED; I HAVE NEVER MET A MISERLY WINE LOVER.

Clifton Fadiman

I RATHER LIKE BAD WINE . . . ONE GETS SO BORED WITH GOOD WINE.

Benjamin Disraeli

WINE-FRIENDLY WASPS

Wasps are a vital component in the wine making process, but not for the reason you might think. Pollination is not the issue, it's the precious yeast. During the summer, the fungus *Saccharomyces cerevisiae* (commonly known as baker's or brewer's yeast) grows on vineyard grapes. If it isn't present while the fruit is growing on the vine, the wine doesn't taste the same; it can't simply be added later. The yeast is killed off by low temperatures but it manages to over-winter in wasp larvae. The wasps eat the grapes, ingest the yeast and regurgitate it for their offspring, so that by the next summer, the next generation of wasps can reintroduce the yeast to the vines.

> GIVE ME BOOKS, FRENCH WINE, FRUIT, FINE WEATHER AND A LITTLE MUSIC PLAYED OUT OF DOORS BY SOMEBODY I DO NOT KNOW.
>
> John Keats

> GO FETCH TO ME A PINT O' WINE.
> AN' FILL IT IN A SILVER TASSIE.
>
> Robert Burns

TASTING NOTES: MERLOT

Dark purplish-red colour

One of the world's most planted grapes (especially in cooler regions). Medium tannin; medium acidity. Often described as lush, voluptuous, plummy, velvety. A typical Merlot will have flavours of plum, blackberry, chocolate, liquorice, mocha, black cherry, jam, but it also offers vanilla, oak, nutmeg. It has a smooth texture and a soft finish. A complex expensive Merlot such as St Emilion, Pomerol or Pétrus will also give you spice, coffee, cinnamon, chocolate, truffle, wet earth and fresh flowers and a velvet silkiness that is unmatched anywhere in Bordeaux.

WINE IS BOTTLED POETRY.

Robert Louis Stevenson

THE FIRST DUTY OF WINE IS TO BE RED ... THE SECOND IS TO BE A BURGUNDY.

Harry Waugh

BACKGROUND MUSIC

Adrian North, Professor of Psychology at Heriot Watt University, was the first person to prove that background music affects the taste of wine. 250 students were each given a glass of either a Cabernet Sauvignon or a Chardonnay, which they drank in one of five rooms. In the first room no music was playing; in the others: 'Powerful and heavy' music – 'Carmina Burana' by Carl Orff; 'subtle and refined' 'Waltz of the Flowers' from *The Nutcracker* by Tchaikovsky; 'zingy and refreshing' 'Just Can't Get Enough' by Nouvelle Vague and 'mellow and soft' 'Slow Breakdown' by Michael Brook. The subjects were then asked to use one of these four categories to describe their wine. Compared to those in the silent room, the ratings of the red and white as 'powerful and heavy' were 60 per cent and 32 per cent higher respectively in the Carmina Burana room; 'subtle and refined' ratings were 41 per cent and 31 per cent higher in the Waltz of the Flowers room; 'zingy and refreshing' ratings were 43 per cent and 40 per cent higher in the Just Can't Get Enough room and 'mellow and soft' ratings were 25 per cent and 26 per cent higher in the Slow Breakdown room.

> THE SCENT OF WINE,
> OH HOW MUCH MORE
> AGREEABLE, LAUGHING,
> PRAYING, CELESTIAL AND
> DELICIOUS IT IS THAN
> THAT OF OIL!
>
> François Rabelais

SUBTLE VIBRATIONS

Chilean winemaker Aurelio Montes plays Gregorian chants to his maturing wines in his Feng Shui-optimised barrel room in the belief that the subtle vibrations improve the quality. His wines also come with music recommendations: Cabernet Sauvignon: 'All Along The Watchtower' (Jimi Hendrix), 'Honky Tonk Women' (Rolling Stones); Chardonnay: 'Atomic' (Blondie), 'Rock DJ' (Robbie Williams); Merlot: 'Sitting On The Dock Of The Bay' (Otis Redding), 'Easy' (Lionel Ritchie); Syrah: 'Nessun Dorma' (Puccini), 'Canon' (Johann Pachelbel).

THIS IS THE GREAT FAULT OF WINE; IT FIRST TRIPS UP THE FEET: IT IS A CUNNING WRESTLER.

Titus Maccius Plautus

WE WANT THE FINEST WINES AVAILABLE TO HUMANITY, WE WANT THEM HERE, AND WE WANT THEM NOW!

Withnail, *Withnail and I*

WINE WITHOUT GRAPES

Japenese saké is probably the best-known non-grape wine, made by fermenting rice that has been polished to remove the bran. Omerto is a Canadian aperitif wine made from tomatoes. In China, tiger bones are steeped in rice wine for up to eight years to make illegal 'Tiger Bone Wine' which costs up to £400 a bottle. *Tezhi Sanbian Jiu* (three-penis wine) can be found in Chinese supermarkets, made from the genitalia of dogs, seals and deer. In South Korea, 'Ttongsul' is a bizarre medicinal rice wine that contains fermented human faeces. Another Korean speciality is 'Baby Mice Wine' which is made by drowning fifteen blind hairless two-day-old mice in a bottle of rice wine and then laying down for twelve months. The resulting concoction is said to taste like petrol, and predictably it is touted for its health-giving properties.

I NEED COFFEE TO HELP ME CHANGE THE THINGS I CAN AND WINE TO HELP ME ACCEPT THE THINGS I CAN'T!

Tanya Masse

> THE WINE ... IT MADE HER LIMBS
> LOOSE AND LIQUID, MADE HER
> FEEL THAT A HUMMINGBIRD HAD
> TAKEN THE PLACE OF HER HEART.
>
> Jodi Picoult

TASTING NOTES: SAUVIGNON BLANC

Sauvignon Blanc is one of the most widely planted wine grapes in the world, but it established its pedigree in Bordeaux and the Loire Valley in France. Its name means 'wild white' and it is notable for its green and herbaceous flavours and its razor-sharp dryness. It has medium-high acidity and its primary fruit flavours are zesty lime, crisp green apple and peach, but look out for bell pepper, grass, fennel, gooseberry, grapefruit, lemon and scores of other herbaceous or fruit flavours.

WORLD BEATERS

The country that collectively consumes the most red wine in the world is China, which accounted for 155 million 9-litre cases in 2013, beating the French into second place by 5 million cases. Red wine is popular in China because red is considered a lucky and prosperous colour. However, the French drink more wine per capita than the Chinese, at 53 litres per person each year, versus 1.9 in China. Inhabitants of Vatican City drink 74 litres each on average, which is the highest per capita figure in the world.

> I COULD SMELL GARLIC, BUTTER, AND WINE ... THE WORLD'S MOST DELICIOUS FLAVOUR COMBINATION. IT MADE ME FEEL WARM, LIKE THE FIRST FEW SIPS OF WINE ALWAYS DO.
>
> Sarah Jio

... THE VERY LEAST ONE REQUIRES FOR CIVILISATION TO SURVIVE IS AN ADEQUATE SUPPLY OF SOUND WINES.

Cynthia Harrod-Eagles

WINE MAKES A MAN ACT LIKE AN ASS IN A RICH PASTURE.

Babur

> WINE IS A SENSUAL PLEASURE.
> ITS REAL VALUE IS WHEN IT
> SPLASHES INTO THE GLASS. IT IS
> NOT IN THE CATEGORY OF A DEGAS
> PAINTING. THE POINT IS NOT FOR
> PEOPLE TO GO TO THEIR CELLAR
> AND STROKE THEIR BOTTLES.
>
> Serena Sutcliffe

GETTING SOAKED

Visitors to the Yunessun Spa Resort in Hakone-Machi, Japan, can swim in red wine. Soaking in red wine is reputed to aid circulation and reduce cellulite. The pool is kept at a constant temperature of 36.6°C and wine pours into it through a giant upturned bottle at set times throughout the day. Some visitors have reported that the air smells like bad farts, probably because of the sulphur dioxide in the wine. There is also a saké pool, a hot green tea pool and a freshly brewed black coffee pool.

THE OLDEST VINE
IN THE WORLD

The oldest grapevine in the world lives in Vojašniška
street in the city of Maribor in Slovenia. Wood samples
have established that 'Old Vine' has a minimum age of
375 years but many believe it was planted in the 1500s.
Paintings of Vojašniška street from the mid-seventeenth
century housed in the Styrian Provincial Museum in
Austria show a mature vine in the same spot. The vine
has survived Napoleon's conquest, two world wars and
today produces a small prized crop of about 50kg of
Žametovka grapes each year, enough to make about one
hundred 250 millilitre bottles, which are reserved as gifts
for dignitaries and important visitors.

> WINE ENHANCES A MEAL. BUT IF
> IT BECOMES A FOCAL POINT, THEN
> MAYBE WE HAVE OUR PRIORITIES
> OUT OF SEQUENCE.
>
> Kelly J Hayes

NOW IS THE TIME FOR DRINKING, NOW THE TIME TO DANCE FOOTLOOSE UPON THE EARTH.

Horace

WINE IS A HIGHLY PERSONAL EXPERIENCE. **YOU MAY LIKE SOMETHING YOUR NEIGHBOUR HATES,** JUST AS WITH FOOD. **YOUR BITTER IS THE NEXT PERSON'S SWEET.**

Catherine Fallis

TASTING NOTES: CABERNET SAUVIGNON

Dark red colour

This grape was created in the 1600s by the accidental natural breeding of Cabernet Franc and Sauvignon Blanc somewhere in southwestern France. Today it is grown in a wide range of climates and produces a robust full-bodied red wine with medium to high tannins and medium acidity so it ages well. Typically expect flavours of dark fruit such as black cherry, blackcurrant, liquorice, black olive and the usual vanilla and oak from the ageing. New World varieties in hotter climates are fruitier, even jammy. The savoury character is often described as black pepper, bell pepper, tobacco, leather. A complex expensive Cabernet Sauvignon such as a Margaux or Inglenook will offer you violets, rose, cassis, truffle and layers of creamy perfumed elegance.

41

> THE MEMORY OF SOME BOTTLES
> CAN STAY WITH YOU FOR LIFE.
> WHILE THE WINE DOESN'T HAVE
> TO BE OLD AND RARE. A GREAT
> OLD BOTTLE CAN BE LIKE A TIME
> CAPSULE. CAPTURING IN ITS
> FLAVOURS AND AROMAS THE TIME
> AND PLACE OF ITS CREATION.

Mireille Guiliano

CHAMPAGNE

Champagne was invented in 1693. Sparkling wine can only be called Champagne if it comes from the region of Champagne, France, which is just outside of Paris, following very specific rules and it only uses a combination of Chardonnay, Pinot Noir and Pinot Meunier grapes.

IN VICTORY, YOU DESERVE CHAMPAGNE. IN DEFEAT YOU NEED IT.

Napoleon Bonaparte

THE BEST WAY TO LEARN ABOUT WINE IS TO UNCORK A FEW BOTTLES AND START SAMPLING.

Harvey Steiman

VINLAND

The Icelandic Norseman Leif Erikson called coastal
North America Vinland ('wine-land' or 'meadow-land')
because of the wide variety of native grapevines
he found there around AD1,000, nearly 500 years
before Columbus 'discovered' the continent.

WINE IS FOR SHARING. WHAT'S THE FUN OF SWIRLING, SWISHING, SLOSHING AND YAKKING IF MY FRIENDS CAN'T JOIN IN?

Jennifer Rosen

45

DIVING FOR CHAMPAGNE

Diver Christian Ekstrom was exploring a shipwreck on the Baltic seabed off the coast of Aaland, part of Finland, when he found thirty bottles of champagne thought to pre-date the French Revolution. He opened a bottle and it was drinkable: 'It was fantastic. It had a very sweet taste, you could taste oak and it had a very strong tobacco smell. And there were very small bubbles'. The champagne is believed to have been made by Clicquot (now Veuve Clicquot) between 1782 and 1788, making it 40 years older than the previous record-holder, a bottle of Perrier-Jouet from 1825.

TOO MUCH OF ANYTHING IS BAD, BUT TOO MUCH CHAMPAGNE IS JUST RIGHT.

Mark Twain

LIFE'S TOO SHORT TO DRINK CHEAP WINE.

Cliff Hakim

POP. GLUG. GLUG. GLUG. CHINK.
AHHH. THESE ARE A FEW OF MY
FAVOURITE NOISES, MARKING AS
THEY DO THE MOST SACRED OF MY
NIGHTLY RITUALS. WINE O'CLOCK.

Helen McGinn

TASTING NOTES: RIESLING

Riesling is grown predominantly in Germany, is famous for
its aromatic flavours and is one of the most collectible wines
in the world (because unlike many whites, a quality Riesling
can be aged for decades). It is light in alcohol and very high
in natural fruity acidity. The aroma is instantly recognisable:
orchard fruits like nectarine, apricot, apple, along with lime
peel, honey, jasmine and that unmistakable whiff of heating
oil (no, you haven't been imagining it and it hasn't been
cut with kerosene – it's a natural compound called TDN –
1,1,6,-trimethyl-1,2-dihydronaphthalene). If you want a dry
Riesling (yes, they do exist), look for 'Trocken' on a German
label, or choose from the Alsace region of France, Austria
and the Finger Lakes region of New York State.

IF YOUR ARTERIES ARE GOOD, EAT MORE ICE CREAM. IF THEY ARE BAD, DRINK MORE RED WINE. PROCEED THUSLY.

Sandra Byrd

... AND ALL WHO SAIL IN HER

The tradition of breaking a bottle of champagne over the prow to launch a ship dates back to the blood sacrifice of Viking times. This had been replaced by wine by the middle ages. Until the late seventeenth century, wine was contained in a cup made of precious metal that was thrown overboard after the ceremony. King William III is reputed to have ended this wasteful practice and made the switch to wine bottles. Using champagne to launch ships became popular during the late nineteenth century.

TITANIC CHRISTENING

A myth has arisen that the bottle of champagne failed to break during the naming ceremony of RMS *Titanic*, presaging ill fortune. In fact, the ship was never christened with champagne because White Star Line didn't christen any of its ships. Despite this, at the beginning of the iconic 1958 film *A Night to Remember*, the ship is duly christened and the champagne bottle breaks first time without a hitch.

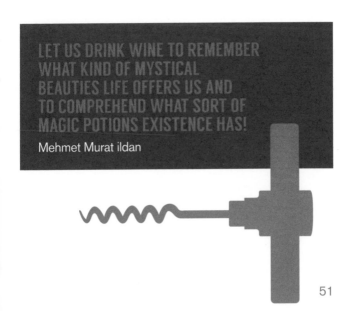

LET US DRINK WINE TO REMEMBER WHAT KIND OF MYSTICAL BEAUTIES LIFE OFFERS US AND TO COMPREHEND WHAT SORT OF MAGIC POTIONS EXISTENCE HAS!

Mehmet Murat ildan

||||||||||||||||||||||||||||||||||||||||||||||||||||||||||||||||||||||||||||||||||||||||||||||||||||||||||||||||||

TASTING NOTES: SYRAH

Deep red-purple colour, pink at the rim

These relatively small grapes produce some of the darkest and most full-bodied red wines in the world. It has medium tannins and acidity, and is often fruit-forward, punching you head on with its bold dark fruit flavours of blackberry, blueberry, then it tails off to a peppery finish. You can also typically expect oak, olive, clove, vanilla, mint, liquorice, chocolate (especially New World), bacon, grilled meat, leather, smoke, tobacco. A complex and expensive Syrah such as Hermitage, Côte-Rôtie or Penfolds Grange will also offer you smoky blackberry, floral notes, herbs and grilled meat.

> GREAT WINES TASTE LIKE THEY COME FROM SOMEWHERE. LESSER WINES TASTE INTERCHANGEABLE: THEY COULD COME FROM ANYWHERE. YOU CAN'T FAKE SOMEWHERENESS.
>
> Matt Kramer

ROMAN FALERNIAN WINE

The best (or the most hyped) wine in Roman times was Falernian, made from grapes grown on the slopes of Mt Massico, 30 miles north of Naples. It even had its own creation myth: a poor humble farmer called Falernus was visited by Bacchus (the Roman god of agriculture, wine and fertility) in disguise. He was so impressed with the farmer's hospitality that he made the cups overflow with wine and when Falernus woke with a hangover the following morning, the whole mountain was blanketed in healthy vines. The best year for Falernian was 121BC. It was such a good year that Romans such as Pliny the Elder were still writing about the vintage two hundred years later. Falernian packed a punch: it was 16 per cent alcohol, although the Romans frequently watered down their wine.

WINE IS A LIVING LIQUID
CONTAINING NO PRESERVATIVES.
ITS LIFE CYCLE COMPRISES
YOUTH, MATURITY, OLD AGE AND
DEATH. WHEN NOT TREATED WITH
REASONABLE RESPECT IT WILL
WEAKEN AND DIE.

Julia Child

TASTING NOTES: PINOT GRIGIO

If you're a fan of supermarket Pinot Grigio, you'll know that it doesn't have a big unique personality, it just quietly gets on with offering its predictable primary fruit flavours of lime, lemon, pear, nectarine, apple. You might occasionally detect floral aromas of honeysuckle or spicy almond or some salty minerality. But chiefly it delivers reliably crisp, tangy dryness and high acidity, but you could be getting so much more. Avoid the supermarket mega brands, go to a proper wine shop and ask the proprietor to recommend a Pinot Grigio to bring some excitement back into your life.

WINE IS OLDER THAN HISTORY. HUMANS DIDN'T INVENT WINE. WE DISCOVERED IT.

Philip Seldon

WHITE WINE IS LIKE ELECTRICITY. RED WINE LOOKS AND TASTES LIKE A LIQUEFIED BEEFSTEAK.

James Joyce

WAITER, THIS WINE IS CORKED

When the waiter or sommelier offers you the cork, he or she is inviting you to inspect its condition. Check that it is neither dry and crumbly nor sodden. It should be intact and free from mould. You can't tell much by smelling it. The sommelier should also keep the bottle facing you so you can check that it's the correct wine and – more importantly – the correct vintage. When tasting, first check the appearance and colour against a white background, then swirl the glass to aerate the wine and release its aroma and bring it to your nose. Take a small sip and roll it around your mouth to check for anything unpleasant in the taste. If the wine is 'corked' it means the cork has contaminated the wine with a compound called 2,4,6-trichloroanisole or TCA, making the wine taste and smell like wet cardboard or even wet dog. It will also have a dry, mouth-puckering finish. If it tastes wrong, ask for another bottle and don't be fobbed off by a snooty, 'it's supposed to be like that'.

TASTING NOTES: GRENACHE

Light, cherry-red colour, semi-translucent

Originally one of the grapes of the Rhône Valley in France, these high-yield grapes are now widely-planted all over the world, so while it arguably finds its finest expression in Châteauneuf-du-Pape, it is just as likely to show up in cheap blended plonk. It has medium tannins and acidity (lighter than a Syrah), though it tends to age rapidly. The fleshy, heady fruits are at the strawberry, raspberry part of the spectrum, but along with the oak ageing, the giveaway flavours are toasty cinnamon and anise. A new stand-out Grenache like Priorat in Spain proves that it can still maintain quality when blended (look out for its distinctive slatey minerality).

> WINE IS LIKE MANY OF THE FINE EXPERIENCES IN LIFE WHICH TAKE TIME AND EXPERIENCE TO EXTRACT THEIR FULL PLEASURE AND MEANING.
>
> Douglas Preston

> IT IS NO COINCIDENCE THAT, ON ALL FOUR SIDES, IN ALL FOUR CORNERS, THE BORDERS OF THE ROMAN EMPIRE STOPPED WHERE WINE COULD NO LONGER BE MADE.
>
> Neel Burton

SUN, SKIN, SOIL

Red wine is made by fermenting crushed grapes and their skins; the skin of white grapes is removed before they are turned into white wine. Since many of the healthy antioxidants are contained in the grape skins, red wine is healthier than white wine. Moderate, regular wine drinking can reduce the risk of heart disease, Alzheimer's disease, stroke and gum disease. Also, as a general rule, the darker the red or more yellow the white wine, the hotter the climate in which the grapes were grown. Hotter climates produce grapes and wines with a richer and more complex taste, but the quality of the soil is also an important factor. Although the soil must be well drained, richly fertile soil is generally not favourable for wine making. Poorer soils tend to produce a more concentrated crop with a more intense flavour.

> IF BACCHUS EVER HAD A
> COLOUR HE COULD CLAIM FOR
> HIS OWN, IT SHOULD SURELY
> BE THE SHADE OF TANNIN ON
> DRUNKEN LIPS, OF JOHN KEATS'
> 'PURPLE STAINED MOUTH', OR
> PERHAPS EVEN OF HOMER'S
> DANGEROUSLY WINE-DARK SEA.
>
> Victoria Finlay

SEAGULL WINE

Although this wine sounds like a sick joke, it's real and was invented by the Inuits. The method is straightforward: stuff a dead seagull into a bottle, fill it with water and leave it outside in the sun to ferment. Drinks blogger Suzanne Donahue describes the taste: 'If you opened up a Toyota's carburettor and drank the leftover fluid from inside, that would be pretty close. It goes down hard and settles in even worse'. The hangover is equally brutal.

WINE IS LIKE THE INCARNATION ... IT IS BOTH DIVINE AND HUMAN.

Paul Tillich

|||||||||||||||||||||||||||||||||||||||||||||||||||||||||||||||||||||||||||||||||||||||||||||||||||||||||||||||||||||||||||||||||||||

TASTING NOTES: CHENIN BLANC

This is a very versatile (some say chameleon) grape, primarily planted in South Africa, the United States and Argentina. There is said to be a Chenin Blanc for any occasion, but for purists, the quintessential old school style can only be found in the Loire Valley in France. It has medium to high acidity but so many possibilities when it comes to flavours: primarily passion fruit, crisp apple, pear, peach depending on the ripeness. In dry wines you'll get lemon, quince, ginger, chamomile, and less dry will give you honeysuckle, jasmine, mango. An oak-aged wine will give you butterscotch, marzipan.

WINE IN THE BIBLE

Wine is the most common alcoholic beverage mentioned in biblical literature. In the Biblical Old Testament, only the Book of Jonah lacks a reference to the vine or wine. The word wine (*yayin*, *tirosh*, *chemer*, etc.) appears about 200 times in the Hebrew Old Testament. There is much wine-based inebriation and admonishment: notoriously Noah planted a vineyard and became drunk and shamed his family by stripping off his clothes.

THIS IS ONE OF THE DISADVANTAGES OF WINE, IT MAKES A MAN MISTAKE WORDS FOR THOUGHTS.

Samuel Johnson

THE JUICE OF THE GRAPE IS THE LIQUID QUINTESSENCE OF CONCENTRATED SUNBEAMS.

Thomas Love Peacock

LAYING DOWN

Not all wines improve with time. In fact, the majority of commercial wines are ready to drink and do not gain much from laying down. Cheap wine will simply get worse. Only medium to high quality wines and those with high tannin content benefit from ageing. Wine should be stored on its side, at a temperature between 8-13° Celsius, in the dark and away from vibrations. Drinking is the only way to tell if a wine is ready to drink.

10,000 VARIETIES OF WINE GRAPES EXIST WORLDWIDE

One acre of grapevines produces approximately 15,940 glasses of wine. One ton of grapes makes about 60 cases of wine, or 720 bottles. One vine can produce between two and three bottles of dry wine, one bottle of wine contains about 1.35 kg of grapes and it takes roughly one cluster of grapes (75–100 grapes) to make one glass.

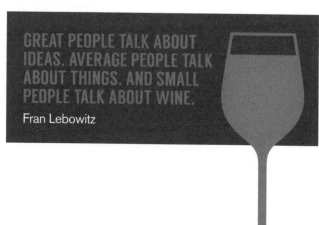

GREAT PEOPLE TALK ABOUT IDEAS. AVERAGE PEOPLE TALK ABOUT THINGS. AND SMALL PEOPLE TALK ABOUT WINE.

Fran Lebowitz

MY ONLY REGRET IN LIFE IS THAT I DIDN'T DRINK ENOUGH CHAMPAGNE.

Robert Noecker

WINE IS THE MOST HEALTHFUL AND MOST HYGIENIC OF BEVERAGES.

Louis Pasteur

TASTING NOTES: SANGIOVESE

Maroon/blood-red colour

Sangiovese (meaning 'Blood of Jove') has always been the dominant grape of central Italian red wines, especially Chianti, but it has only recently thrown off its association with overcropping and cheap, tart Italian reds. Also, despite high tannin and acidity, it has a reputation for going brown quickly. Expect violet aromas, then the dominant fruit is usually cherry, redcurrants, strawberry, fig. There are many varieties of the vine, so the earthier savoury components can range from roasted pepper and tomato to dark chocolate, leather and tobacco; oregano and roses, along with light oak ageing. A bottle of Vino Nobile di Montepulciano or Brunello di Montalcino is a reliable way to explore the complexity of this Tuscan grape (known locally as *Prugnolo Gentile*).

SEASONING OR POISON?

Ancient Romans routinely seasoned their wine with fermented fish sauce, garlic, asafetida (onion root), absinthe and even lead acetate (which today is used in hair colouring products), which they called *sapa* and used to sweeten the wine. This has lead some historians to claim that widespread lead poisoning contributed to the decline of the Roman Empire. Wine was also sweetened with honey to make 'Mulsum', which was served as an aperitif.

WINE IS LIKE SEX IN THAT FEW MEN WILL ADMIT NOT KNOWING EVERYTHING ABOUT IT.

Hugh Johnson

QUICKLY, BRING ME A BEAKER OF WINE, SO THAT I MAY WET MY MIND AND SAY SOMETHING CLEVER.

Aristophanes

WHAT I LIKE TO DRINK MOST IS WINE THAT BELONGS TO OTHERS.

Diogenes

HOUSE OF ARCANE DELIGHTS

According to a Freedom of Information request, MPs and other guests to the tax-payer subsidised bars and restaurants of the House of Commons in Westminster, London, guzzled 42,711 bottles of wine and champagne and 6,000 bottles of gin in 2015-16, which was triple the amount consumed two years previously. The total bill for all this booze was £1.8 million.

WHAT IS BETTER THAN TO SIT AT THE END OF A DAY AND DRINK WINE WITH FRIENDS, OR SUBSTITUTE FOR FRIENDS.

James Joyce

TASTING NOTES: MUSCAT/MOSCATO

One of the oldest grapes in the world, it is famous for its sweet low alcohol wine with primary flavours of peach, orange and nectarine. It grows everywhere but hails from Italy, although its name is most likely Persian. It has a distinctive 'Muscat' aroma which scientists have recently identified as a chemical group called monoterpenes, especially linalool which is also found in mint, rosewood, citrus fruits and birch trees. Among the many types of Muscat grapes, Muscat Blanc à Petits Grains is the primary variety used in the production of the Italian sparkling wine Asti (Moscato Asti) in the Piedmont region.

> THE DISCOVERY OF A WINE
> IS OF GREATER MOMENT
> THAN THE DISCOVERY OF A
> CONSTELLATION. THE UNIVERSE
> IS TOO FULL OF STARS.
>
> Benjamin Franklin

THE MARGAUX IS ALL MINE

It is well known that the disgraced former 37th President of the United States, Richard Nixon, was a big fan of Château Margaux wine. Some say that he refused to drink anything else. It is lesser known that when he dined with guests, he served them inferior wine but ordered the waiter to wrap his own bottle in a tea towel to disguise his greed and selfishness.

CLASSIFICATION OF CHAMPAGNE BOTTLE SIZES

Type	Capacity	Bottle Equivalent	Number of Glasses
Piccolo	18.75 cl	1/4	1
Demi	37.5 cl	1/2	3
Bottle	75 cl	1	6
Magnum	1.5 l	2	12
Jeroboam	3 l	4	24
Rehoboam	4.5 l	6	36
Methuselah	6 l	8	48
Salmanazar	9 l	12	72
Balthazar	12 l	16	96
Nebuchadnezzar	15 l	20	120
Solomon	18 l	24	144
Sovereign	25 l	34	200
Primat	27 l	36	216
Melchizedek	30 l	40	240

A JEROBOAM OF CHAMPAGNE IS PRESENTED TO THE WINNER OF A GRAND PRIX MOTOR RACE. THE TRADITION OF SPRAYING THE CROWD AROSE BY ACCIDENT IN 1966 AFTER SWISS DRIVER JO SIFFERT WON THE 24 HOURS OF LE MANS RACE. HE WAS GIVEN A BOTTLE OF CHAMPAGNE THAT HAD BEEN LEFT OUT IN THE SUN, SO IT SPRAYED UNINTENTIONALLY. THE FOLLOWING YEAR, WHEN CALIFORNIAN RACER DAN GURNEY WON LE MANS, HE DELIBERATELY COPIED SIFFERT AND ESTABLISHED THE TRADITION.

WE ARE ALL MORTAL UNTIL THE FIRST KISS AND THE SECOND GLASS OF WINE.

Eduardo Galeano

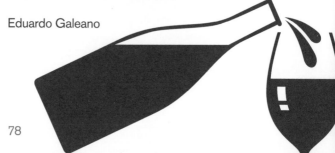

> ONE SHOULD ALWAYS BE DRUNK.
> THAT'S ALL THAT MATTERS ...
> BUT WITH WHAT? WITH WINE,
> WITH POETRY, OR WITH VIRTUE,
> AS YOU CHOSE. BUT GET DRUNK.
>
> Charles Baudelaire

TASTING NOTES: NEBBIOLO

Brick-red, translucent, orange at the rim

This fastidious grape originally hails from the region of Piedmont in north-west Italy where it stars in Barolo and Barbaresco wines. Its translucent colour belies its full-bodied flavour with high tannin and acidity. It is famously highly aromatic, with a bouquet of roses, violets and autumn leaves. The dominant fruit flavours are typically cherry, raspberry, cranberry, fruitcake, accompanied by earthier elements of clove, anise, leather, wood smoke, tar, red clay. It can be velvety if sufficiently aged. Also check out Gattinara and Ghemme as well as some of the less pricey Piemonte wines.

ANTIOXIDANTS

The naturally occurring polyphenols called tannins that give red wine its complex flavour and longevity are only produced by the grape to protect the vine from caterpillars. In fact, red wine contains so many organic compounds that it is considered more complex than blood serum. One glass of red wine provides the same antioxidant benefits as twenty glasses of apple juice or seven glasses of orange juice. Wines from the island of Sardinia and those from the southwest of France have been found to contain higher levels of certain health-enhancing tannins (procyanidins) than wines from other regions and countries.

> WINE GIVES A MAN NOTHING. IT NEITHER GIVES HIM KNOWLEDGE NOR WIT: IT ONLY ANIMATES A MAN, AND ENABLES HIM TO BRING OUT WHAT A DREAD OF THE COMPANY HAS REPRESSED.
>
> Samuel Johnson

IN THE MIDDLE OF THE NIGHT YOU WAKE UP. YOU START TO CRY. WHAT'S HAPPENING TO ME? OH, MY LIFE, OH, MY YOUTH ... THERE'S SOME WINE LEFT IN THE BOTTLE. YOU DRINK IT. THE CLOCK TICKS. SLEEP ...

Jean Rhys

TASTING NOTES: GEWÜRZTRAMINER

This grape only enjoys about 20,000 acres worldwide, even though it is one of the original 'cépages nobles' and one of the four Grand Cru grapes of Alsace. It has been described as a grown-up version of Muscat (higher alcohol, lower acidity and more powerful aromatics). The main flavour ranges from grapefruit through lychee to pineapple depending on ripeness. In fact, it is this lychee aroma (sweet rose) that gives away the grape in a blind tasting and also fools you into thinking it is sweeter to taste. Unfortunately, most Gewürztraminer today is wasted in low quality supermarket sweet wine, which is why so many people try it once and never revisit. However, a top-rated Gewürztraminer will give you lots of complex aromatics including rose petal, ginger, lemon oil, cloves, cinnamon, honey and a sweet smoky incense.

> I DRANK A BOTTLE OF WINE FOR
> COMPANY. IT WAS CHÂTEAU
> MARGAUX. IT WAS PLEASANT TO
> BE DRINKING SLOWLY AND TO BE
> TASTING THE WINE AND TO BE
> DRINKING ALONE. A BOTTLE OF
> WINE WAS GOOD COMPANY.
>
> Ernest Hemingway

HANGING ON THE WALL

The dark green or brown wine bottle was an English invention, the brainchild of Sir Kenelm Digby (1603-1665), a courtier, diplomat, privateer and founding member of the Royal Society. During the 1630s he owned a glassworks and pioneered a technique to manufacture a bottle that was stronger than most of its contemporaries, with a dark colour to protect the contents. He also tried to invent a 'powder of sympathy' that could cure people by being rubbed on the object that had caused the injury.

TO TAKE WINE INTO OUR MOUTHS IS TO SAVOUR A DROPLET OF THE RIVER OF HUMAN HISTORY.

Clifton Fadiman

CORKS

About one third of the world's wine bottle corks are made from cork grown in Portugal. There are 2,200,000 hectares of cork forest worldwide. Cork is the most eco-friendly wine stopper; cork trees live 200 years and can be harvested from early May to late August every nine years, once they reach 25 years of age. The almost impermeable substance in cork that gives it its waxy rubbery texture is called suberin. Before cork, wine bottles were sealed with oil-soaked rags.

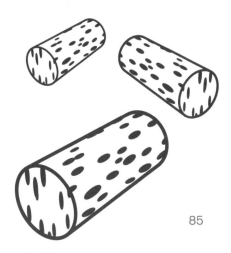

TASTING NOTES: TEMPRANILLO

Medium ruby to medium garnet colour, translucent

This ancient black grape variety is widely grown to make full-bodied red wines in its native Spain, and is the dominant grape of red Rioja as well as fruitier, less earthy wines in the New World. It has medium tannin and acidity and is sometimes described as having a predominantly savoury rather than sweet taste. A quality Tempranillo will balance fruit flavours of cherry, plum, tomato and dried fig, with leather, tobacco, cedar and vanilla; much less oak nowadays allows the grape to speak for itself. It typically has a smooth finish with plenty of tannin.

A WINE IS READY WHEN YOU CAN'T BEAR TO WAIT FOR IT ANY LONGER.

Karen MacNeil

TASTEVIN

A 'tastevin' is a tiny shallow silver tasting cup, commonly worn on a chain around the neck and used by wine tasters and producers of old. It is concave, shiny and multifaceted, allowing connoisseurs to assess the colour and clarity of the wine in dim candle-lit wine cellars. Their use all but died out after the French Revolution and the introduction of gas and electric lighting, but some modern day sommeliers still wear them as an affectation.

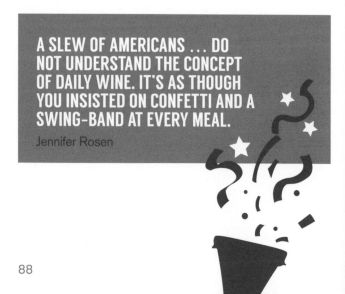

A SLEW OF AMERICANS ... DO NOT UNDERSTAND THE CONCEPT OF DAILY WINE. IT'S AS THOUGH YOU INSISTED ON CONFETTI AND A SWING-BAND AT EVERY MEAL.

Jennifer Rosen

PRODUCTION OF WINE IN THE WORLD

(in 1,000s hectolitres)

1. France (57,386)
2. Italy (53,000)
3. Spain (42,988)
4. USA (20,169)
5. Russia (12,386)
6. Argentina (15,464)
7. Australia (13,811)
8. China (11,700)

...

40. UK (17)

TASTING NOTES: SÉMILLON

Sémillon is France's third most planted white wine grape behind Sauvignon Blanc and Chardonnay. It has medium to low acidity and its primary fruit flavours are zippy lemon, fresh apple, pear, papaya and mango depending on the ripeness, but it also has a distinctive waxy taste. Other aromas include honeysuckle, saffron, hay, ginger and buttery oak if aged well. It is commonly blended with Sauvignon Blanc and Muscadelle in White Bordeaux and is the main ingredient in 'Noble Rot' dessert wines.

WINE TALKS. EVERYONE KNOWS THAT. LOOK AROUND YOU. ASK THE ORACLE AT THE STREET CORNER: THE UNINVITED GUEST AT THE WEDDING FEAST: THE HOLY FOOL. IT TALKS.

Joanne Harris

ROSÉ IS NOT JUST A MIX OF RED AND WHITE WINE

To make rosé wine, the skin of red grapes is immersed in the wine for a short time (from 2 to 20 hours). The longer the skins are left to soak, the deeper pink the colour. Rosé is not a wine for laying down. It should be consumed within two to three years of purchase.

WIMBLEDON CHAMPAGNE DRINKING CHAMPIONSHIPS

The House of Lanson has been making Champagne since 1760 with a perfect balance of fruitiness, elegance and freshness. It has been an official supplier of the Wimbledon Lawn Tennis Championships since 2001. Each year over 28,000 bottles of Lanson Champagne are consumed during the two-week event.

> OCCASIONALLY I HAVE A GLASS
> OF RED WINE. I DON'T CONSIDER
> IT AN ALCOHOLIC DRINK.
> I CONSIDER IT A HOLY DRINK,
> SOMETHING THAT CAN ALSO BE
> USED AS A CURATIVE.
>
> Novak Djokovic

TASTING NOTES: MALBEC

Deep purple-red colour, magenta-tinged rim

Malbec grows mostly in Argentina and produces a full-bodied, dark, fruit-forward red wine with medium tannin and acidity. You'll get red cherry and raspberry flavours in the cooler climates, and blackberry, black cherry and plum in the warmer growing areas. In France, expect higher acidity, pepper and spice with flavours of tart currant. A high-quality Malbec will offer lots of nuanced notes including violet, chocolate, cocoa powder, leather, with a sweet tobacco finish.

GRAPE BRICKS

During the US Prohibition era (1920-33), winemakers faced a tough choice. No one knew how long the alcohol ban would last, so if they ripped out their vines to plant a different crop, it could take another decade to re-grow mature vines once the ban was lifted. US law only allowed the cultivation of grapes for non-alcoholic consumption, but vineyards could legally manufacture grape bricks with an explicit warning that on no account should customers dissolve the concentrate in a gallon of water then leave in a cool cupboard for 21 days, because that would make it turn into wine.

TASTING NOTES: VIOGNIER

This full-bodied white wine grape originated in southern France. It is famed for its perfume aroma of peach, tangerine and honeysuckle, but it can also develop bold creamy vanilla notes when oak-aged, as well as nutmeg and clove. With medium acidity and high alcohol content, it's like a Chardonnay, with a more delicate perfume and citrus floral notes, a softer start and a more bitter, almond finish, with the buttery oiliness in the middle rather than at the end.

> BEFORE I WAS MARRIED I LEARNED THE DIFFERENCE BETWEEN A CHEAP AND EXPENSIVE WINE. AFTER I WAS MARRIED I LEARNED TO DRINK THE CHEAP WINE.
>
> Paul Smith

OAK AGEING

Wine had been stored in clay jars known as amphorae by the Romans (and the Greeks before them) for centuries until they encountered the Galls of Northern Europe, who stored their beer in oak barrels. Oak was abundant, it was easier to bend than the palm wood used to make barrels in parts of the Mediterranean, plus its tight grain made it waterproof. The Romans recognised an innovation when they saw one, when they made the switch from clay to oak for transportation, they also discovered the added pleasure of oaked wine. So began the practice of ageing wine in oak.

TASTING NOTES: ZINFANDEL

Deep red, translucent

The black-skinned Zinfandel grape is most widely grown in California, although it originally hailed from Croatia, where it has been known as Tribidrag since at least the 15th century. It arrived in the US via the Imperial Nursery in Vienna, Austria, in the early 1800s. It has medium-high tannin and acidity and the spicy/candied fruit flavour ranges from strawberry to blackberry depending on the climate and ripeness. Oak-aged varieties offer cloves, cinnamon, liquorice, mocha, Asian 5 Spice, with a sweet tobacco smoky finish. Despite the grape's complexity, today about 85 per cent of production goes to make the popular sweet Rosé known as White Zinfandel.